Playful Pandas

Growing Up Wild

Madison Parker

Norwood House Press

Cataloging-in-Publication Data

Names: Parker, Madison.
Title: Playful pandas / Madison Parker.
Description: Buffalo, NY : Norwood House Press, 2026. | Series: Growing up wild | Includes glossary and index.
Identifiers: ISBN 9781978574175 (pbk.) | ISBN 9781978574182 (library bound) | ISBN 9781978574199 (ebook)
Subjects: LCSH: Pandas--Infancy--Juvenile literature. | Pandas--Juvenile literature.
Classification: LCC QL737.C27 P375 2026 | DDC 599.78913'92--dc23

Published in 2026 by
Norwood House Press
2544 Clinton Street
Buffalo, NY 14224

Designer: Rhea Magaro
Editor: Kim Thompson

Photo credits: Cover, p. 1 Wonderly Imaging/Shutterstock.com; p. 5 Hung Chung Chi /Shutterstock.com; p. 6 Earth Picture Galleries /Shutterstock.com; pp. 8, 9 Foreverhappy /Shutterstock.com; p. 11 Oakdalecch/Dreamstime.com; p. 13 dangdumrong /Shutterstock.com; p. 14 Daniel X D /Shutterstock.com; p. 15 Danny Ye/ Shutterstock.com; p. 17 Elen Marlen /Shutterstock.com; pp. 18, 19 Ondrej Prosicky; p. 21 Japan's Fireworks /Shutterstock.com;

Printed in the United States of America

CPSIA compliance information: Batch #CSNHP26: For further information contact Norwood House Press at 1-800-237-9932.

TABLE OF CONTENTS

Playful Pandas

Pandas grow up in the **wild**. Baby pandas are called cubs.

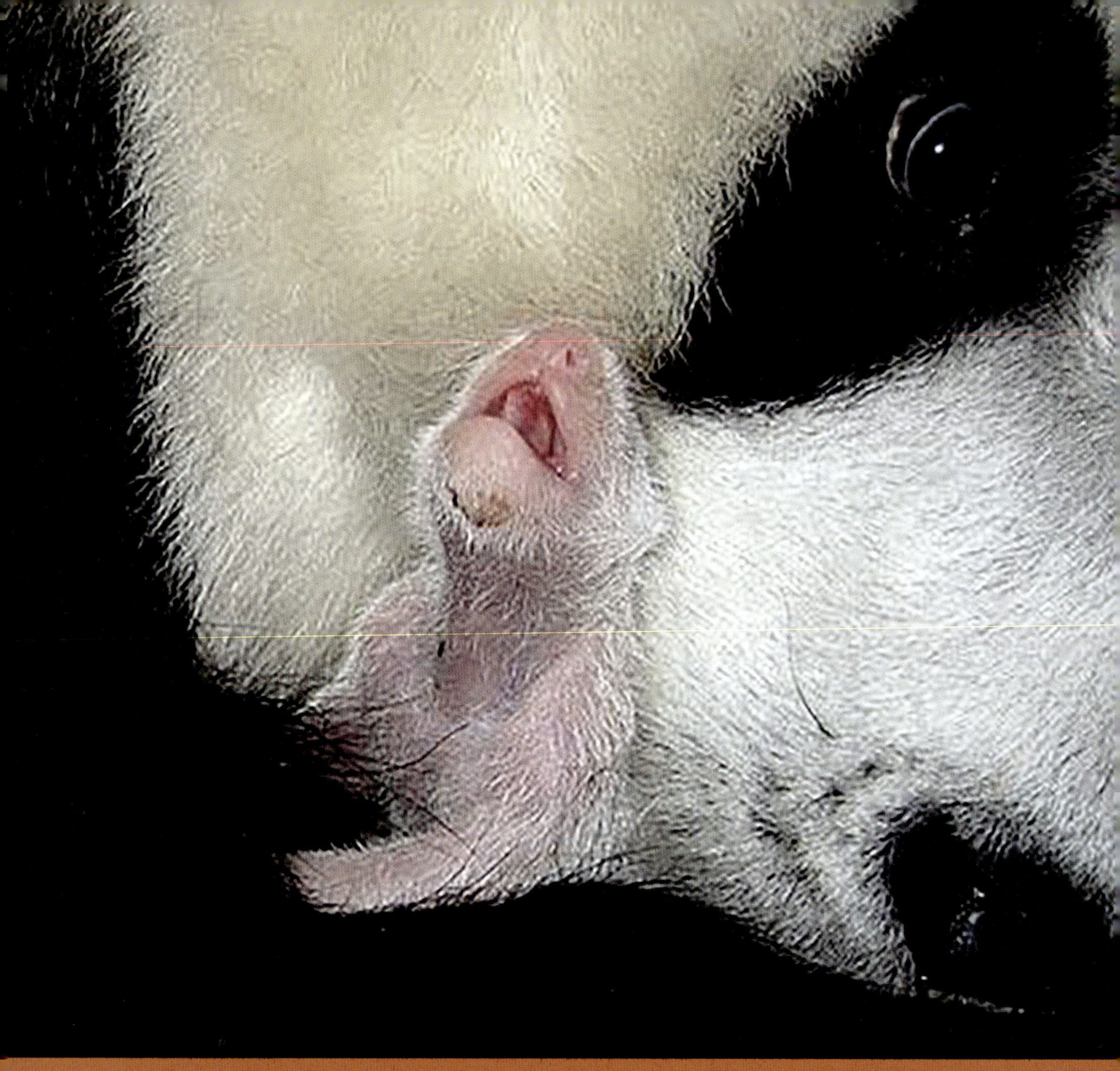

How Baby Pandas Look

When cubs are born, they are tiny and pink. They have no teeth. They cannot see, hear, or crawl.

Baby pandas grow fast. Their eyes open. Black and white fur covers their skin.

Panda cubs have four short legs. They have **claws** on each paw.

How Baby Pandas Sound

Baby pandas make sounds to **communicate**. They squeal and **grunt**.

They **bleat** to call their mothers. They honk when they are upset.

What Baby Pandas Eat

Panda cubs drink milk from their mothers. When they are about five months old, they try other foods.

Pandas are **omnivores**. They mostly eat **bamboo**. Sometimes, they eat meat.

Baby pandas grow teeth. They chew on bamboo stems. They munch on leaves.

Lots to Learn

Panda cubs crawl when they are about three months old. Soon, they learn to walk. Cubs **wrestle** and play with their mothers.

Baby pandas explore the forest.

They climb trees.

They learn to find food on their own.

All Grown Up

When it is about 18 months old, a young panda is **mature**. It is ready to leave its mother and find its own **territory**.

Glossary

bamboo (bam-BOO): a tropical plant with a hollow, woody stem

bleat (bleet): to make a sharp cry

claws (klawz): sharp, curved nails on the feet of animals

communicate (kuh-MYOO-ni-kate): to share information and feelings

grunt (gruhnt): to make a short, low sound

mature (muh-CHOOR): fully grown or developed; adult

omnivores (AHM-nuh-vorz): animals that eat both plants and meat

territory (TER-i-tor-ee): an area of land that an animal claims as its home

wild (wilde): natural places where no people live

wrestle (RES-uhl): to playfully fight and struggle

Thinking Questions

1. What are baby pandas called?
2. Name three body parts baby pandas have.
3. How does a panda cub change as it grows up?
4. What do pandas eat?
5. At what age do young pandas leave their mothers?

Index

About the Author

Madison Parker spent her childhood in the city of Chicago, Illinois. A farm girl at heart, today she lives in Wisconsin with her husband and four children on a small farm with cows, goats, chickens, and two miniature horses named Harley and David. Her favorite dessert is vanilla frozen custard with rainbow sprinkles, even in the winter.